A Guide for Using

The

Pearl

in the Classroom

Based on the novel written by John Steinbeck

*This guide written by **Philip Denny***

Teacher Created Materials, Inc.
6421 Industry Way
Westminster, CA 92683
www.teachercreated.com
© *1992 Teacher Created Materials, Inc.*
Reprinted, 2002
Printed in U.S.A.

ISBN 1-55734-407-8

Edited by
Ina Massler Levin

Illustrated by
Sue Fullam

Table of Contents

Introduction

A good book can touch our lives like a good friend. Within its pages are words and characters that can inspire us to achieve our highest ideals. We can turn to it for companionship, recreation, comfort, and guidance. It also gives us a cherished story to hold in our hearts forever.

In Literature Units, great care has been taken to select books that are sure to become good friends!

Teachers who use this literature unit will find the following features to supplement their own valuable ideas.

- Sample Lesson Plans

- Pre-reading Activities

- A Biographical Sketch and Picture of the Author

- A Book Summary

- Vocabulary Lists and Suggested Vocabulary Activities

- Chapters grouped for study, with each section including:

   —*quizzes*

   —*hands-on projects*

   —*cooperative learning activities*

   —*cross-curriculum connections*

   —*extensions into the reader's own life*

- Post-reading Activities

- Book Report Ideas

- Research Ideas

- A Culminating Activity

- Three Different Options for Unit Tests

- Bibliography

- Answer Key

We are confident that this unit will be a valuable addition to your planning, and hope that as you use our ideas, your students will increase the circle of "friends" that they can have in books!

Sample Lesson Plan

Each of the lessons suggested below can take from one to several days to complete.

LESSON 1
- Introduce and complete some or all of the pre-reading activities found on page 5.
- Read "About the Author" with your students. (page 6)
- Read the book summary with your students. (page 7)
- Introduce vocabulary list for Section 1. (page 8)

LESSON 2
- Read chapters I - II. As you read, place the vocabulary words in the context of the story and discuss their meanings.
- Do a vocabulary activity. (page 9)
- Create your American Dream. (page 11)
- Do Science: Poison. (page 13)
- Find examples of imagery. (page 12)
- Begin "Reading Response Journals." (page 14)
- Administer Section 1 Quiz. (page 10)
- Introduce vocabulary list for Section 2. (page 8)

LESSON 3
- Read Chapter III. Place the vocabulary words in the context of the story and discuss their meanings.
- Do a vocabulary activity. (page 9)
- Do the characterization exercises. (page 16)
- Characterize classmates. (page 17)
- Discuss the book in terms of science. (page 18)
- Complete There Ought To Be a Law. (page 19)
- Administer Section 2 Quiz. (page 15)
- Introduce vocabulary list for Section 3. (page 8)

LESSON 4
- Read Chapter IV. Place the vocabulary words in the context of the story and discuss their meanings.
- Do a vocabulary activity. (page 9)
- Plan for A Dream Come True. (page 21)
- Do a writing activity. (page 22)
- Discuss the book in terms of math. (page 23)
- Create The "Right" Look. (page 24)

- Administer Section 3 Quiz. (page 20)
- Introduce vocabulary list for Section 4. (page 8)

LESSON 5
- Read Chapter V. Place the vocabulary words in context and discuss all possible meanings.
- Do a vocabulary activity. (page 9)
- Become a reporter. (page 26)
- Become a detective. (page 27)
- Discuss the book in terms of geography. (page 28)
- Do some problem solving. (page 29)
- Administer Section 4 Quiz. (page 25)
- Introduce vocabulary list for Section 5. (page 8)

LESSON 6
- Read Chapter VI. Place the vocabulary words in context and discuss all possible meanings.
- Practice writing personification. (page 31)
- Do a vocabulary activity. (page 9)
- Personify through art. (page 32)
- Discuss the book in terms of science. (page 33)
- Test your survival skills. (page 34)
- Administer Section 5 Quiz. (page 30)

LESSON 7
- Discuss any questions the students may have about the story. (page 35)
- Assign book report. (page 36)
- Begin work on culminating activities: essay and book cover. (pages 38, 39, 40, and 41)

LESSON 8
- Administer one, two, and/or three unit tests. (pages 42, 43, and 44)
- Discuss the test answers and possibilities.
- Discuss the students' enjoyment of the book.
- Provide a list of related reading for your students. (page 45)

Before the Book

Before you begin reading *The Pearl* with your students, do some pre-reading activities to stimulate interest and enhance comprehension. Here are some activities that might work well in your class.

1. Predict what the story might be about just by hearing the title.

2. Predict what the story might be about just by looking at the cover illustration.

3. Discuss other books by John Steinbeck that students may have heard about or read.

4. Answer these questions

    • Are you interested in: :

        __ stories involving different cultures?

        __ stories that have a treasure involved?

        __ stories that have increasing suspense?

        __ stories that have an involved plot?

    • Would you ever:

        __ take a risk to reach a goal?

        — fight to defend members of your family?

        — take a stand even though the whole community seems to be against you?

        — sacrifice members of your own family just so you could succeed?

    • Have you ever met a person who was so strong-willed that he/she became blind to the consequences of his/her actions? Describe your experiences with that person.

5. Work in groups or as a class to create your own story about taking great risks to find and possess a treasure.

6. So that students will be able to watch for examples, teach a lesson on foreshadowing, a writing technique used by authors to give hints and clues about what is going to happen in the story. Use examples from *The Pearl,* such as the scene where Kino is reluctant to open the very large, ancient oyster (near the end of Chapter II).

7. Use a picture of a gleaming pearl in its open shell (page 48) to help introduce *The Pearl* to your class. The picture can also be used as a journal cover or the centerpiece of a bulletin board display of student work.

About the Author

John Steinbeck was born in Salinas, California on February 27, 1902, to Olive and John Ernst Steinbeck. His parents were both educated professionals. His father was the Treasurer of Monterey County and his mother a teacher. Due to his mother's influence, John Steinbeck became an avid reader early in his life. He loved classics, such as *Robin Hood,* and books on the Crusades. Perhaps these early reading experiences influenced him later in his own novels, where he championed the underprivileged.

His books are filled with commentary that makes clear the social extremes of life. He balances the oppression of the world's "have-nots" with imagery of the small, everyday joys of life.

Many of his books are set around California's Monterey coast, where Steinbeck grew up. The bay at Monterey, the tide pools, and the sea life fed his imagination. His novel, *Cannery Row,* actually takes place in Monterey, while *The Pearl* uses descriptive images of the sea.

In his boyhood, Steinbeck excelled in athletics, especially track and basketball. After high school, he briefly attended Stanford University, where, in 1920, he wrote several short stories and poems which he submitted to the school's literary clubs. He left the university to become a reporter in New York City.

In 1929 Steinbeck returned to California to take up writing seriously. His first novel was published that year. This novel was merely a longer version of one which he wrote at Stanford. Nevertheless, it sent him headlong into the literary world. He wrote many successful novels throughout his lifetime, but perhaps none was more significant than *The Grapes of Wrath,* published in 1939. This book won great respect for Steinbeck, and he was awarded the Pulitzer Prize. Like *The Pearl,* this book documents the exploitation of the poor.

Before his death in 1968, Steinbeck lived in the New York area. He had an apartment in the city, but he spent much of his time in a cottage nestled on a secluded two acres near Long Island's Sag Harbor. He continued writing there in a workshop, which he designed himself, enjoying its Spartan simplicity.

Several of his novels are still required reading in high schools and colleges around the country, as they are considered classics that have endured the test of time.

6

The Pearl

By John Steinbeck

(Bantam, 1945, 1974)

The setting of *The Pearl* is a small, sleepy, Mexican fishing village named La Paz nestled on an estuary of the Gulf of California. It is, on the surface, a simple story told with simple, clear, picturesque language. You do not have to get far into the novel, though, to discover that, like a pearl, there is layer upon layer of meaning to this unique story.

The Pearl tells how a "lucky" fisherman, Kino, discovers the Pearl of the World. The rest of the story deals with how he attempts to cash the pearl in and obtain a better life for his family.

Kino's original well-wishers turn on him. Like the town itself, Kino is blind to the poison of greed which infects him. Unknown "dark" people attempt to steal his pearl. There are attacks on Kino which cause him harm and ultimately result in death.

In this story a fisherman, who has led a tranquil life, tries to rise above his station. It tells of the society with which he comes in conflict. Throughout the story, the author shows us a society built on prejudice and greed. This is a society that has no intention of allowing an outsider, an underprivileged person, to realize the dream of bettering his life. This society is determined to hold him down. In the end, Kino realizes that the pearl has brought no guarantees of a better life, because peace and happiness cannot be bought.

Vocabulary

On this page are vocabulary lists which correspond to each sectional grouping of chapters. Vocabulary activity ideas can be found on page 9 of this book. Vocabulary knowledge may be evaluated by including selected words in the quizzes and tests. This can be done with matching, multiple choice, or fill-in-the-blank questions.

SECTION 1
Chapters I-II

blustered	obscured
detachment	oysters
determination	pearl
discontent	poultice
estuary	puncture
feinted	reassuring
flagstones	scorpion
instinctive	strenuous
lymphatic	ulcers

SECTION 2
Chapter III

anxiety	luxurious
carbine	namesake
confirmation	nervous system
disparagement	precipitate
distillate	prophecy
emotion	recount
guidance	semblance
horizon	speculation
judicious	transfigured
lucent	visualize

SECTION 3
Chapter IV

assaults	irresponsible
clustered	perplexed
communication	procession
contemptuous	rash
crevices	self-conscious
dignity	solemn
experiment	stalwart
extravagant	swabbed
hibiscus	understatement

SECTION 4
Chapter V

conceived	mangroves
crouched	misfortune
exhilaration	plunged
formal	preservation
glinted	rage
greedy	retrieving
insane	scuttling
lament	searing
leprosy	sluggish

SECTION 5
Chapter VI

Cautious	pelted
cleft	resin
desert	rutted
feverish	shimmering
goading	slouching
guttural	spurs
lumbered	strayed
monolithic	symbolic
monotonously	triumphant
panic	warning

8

Vocabulary Activity Ideas

You can help your students learn and retain the vocabulary in *The Pearl* by providing them with interesting vocabulary activities. Here are a few ideas to try.

❏ People of all ages like to make and solve puzzles. Ask your students to make their own **Crossword Puzzles** or **Wordsearch Puzzles** using the vocabulary words from the story.

❏ Challenge your students to a **Vocabulary Bee**. This is similar to a spelling bee, but in addition to spelling each word correctly, the game participants must correctly define the words as well.

❏ Play **Vocabulary Concentration**. The goal of this game is to match vocabulary words with their definitions. Divide the class into groups of 2–5 students. Have students make two sets of cards the same size and color. On one set have them write the vocabulary words. On the second set have them write the definitions. All cards are mixed together and placed face down on a table. A player picks two cards. If the pair matches the word with its definition, the player keeps the cards and takes another turn. If the cards don't match, they are returned to their places face down on the table, and another player takes a turn. Player must concentrate to remember the locations of words and their definitions. The game continues until all matches have been made. This is an ideal activity for free exploration time.

❏ Have your students practice their writing skills by creating sentences and paragraphs in which multiple vocabulary words are used correctly. Ask them to share their **Compact Vocabulary** sentences and paragraphs with the class.

❏ Ask your students to create paragraphs which use the vocabulary words to present **Science and Geographical Lessons** that relate to the events mentioned in the story.

❏ Challenge your students to use a specific vocabulary word from the story at least **Ten Times in One Day**. They must keep a record of when, how, and why the word was used.

❏ As a group activity, have students work together to create an **Illustrated Dictionary** of the vocabulary words.

❏ Play **20 Clues** with the entire class. In this game, one student selects a vocabulary word and gives clues about this word, one by one, until someone in the class can guess the word.

❏ Play **Vocabulary Charades**. In this game, vocabulary words are acted out.

You probably have many more ideas to add to this list. Try them! See if experiencing vocabulary on a personal level increases your students' vocabulary interest and retention.

Quiz

1. On the back of this paper, write a one paragraph summary of the major events in each chapter of this section. Then complete the rest of the questions on this page.

2. Early in the first chapter, the author introduces the reader to songs. What does the "Song of the Family" mean for Kino?

   _____

   _____

3. Foreshadowing is a technique an author uses to give clues about future events that will take place in the story. What was the song that hinted that evil was about to interrupt Kino's family?

   _____

4. The author writes that "It was a morning like other mornings" as Kino awaits his breakfast. Briefly describe their morning, before breakfast.

   _____

5. Why do you suppose the author chose the word "delicately" when he wrote: "The scorpion moved delicately down the rope" to Coyotito's box?

   _____

   _____

6. What surprising thing did Juana do after Coyotito was stung by the scorpion?

   _____

   _____

7. What are some of the differences between Kino's neighborhood and that of the doctor?

   _____

8. How does the author describe of character the doctor?

   _____

9. Kino went to the doctor for help, yet the author writes that Kino could "kill the doctor more easily than he could talk to him." Explain this seeming contradiction.

   _____

   _____

10. The doctor informs his servant that he has no time to "cure insect bites for little Indians" and that he is not a "veterinary" doctor. What new element is added here to his character?

   _____

The American Dream

There are several elements involved in "The American Dream." Generally speaking, it is the ability to attain the "good life." This might include owning your own house, having enough money so that you and your family can enjoy leisure time together, and giving your children the opportunity to go to college and have a better life themselves.

Kino's world is quite different from those who live in the "city of stone." The doctor, for instance, enjoys his breakfast of sweet biscuits and hot chocolate in his private chambers surrounded by high outer walls and "cool inner gardens" with the "splash of cooling water" bubbling in the fountains. Kino, on the other hand, merely "squatted by the fire pit and rolled a hot corncake and dipped it in a sauce" while inside a single room brush house.

As Steinbeck describes the trip of Kino's family to the doctor, he shows that the reasons for these differences in lifestyle are twofold—poverty and prejudice. Kino's poverty is shown, for example, when the beggars in front of the church note the poorness of the family's clothes and by the fact that Kino has no money to pay the doctor. But it is not only the lack of money that causes the doctor to refuse treatment. He is obviously prejudiced against Indians whom he considers little better than animals, as evidenced when he says, " 'Have I nothing better to do than cure insect bites for "little Indians"? I am a doctor, not a veterinary.' "

In our own society there are vast differences between the "haves" and the "have-nots" as well. Kino's big break in reaching his dream is the finding of the pearl. This would be similar to someone in our society winning a once-in-a-lifetime lottery.

From Dream To Reality

What would you include as essential in your American Dream?

In a paragraph, tell where you would live and describe your life in this dream.

- List as many ways as possible to insure that you reach this goal.

- Discuss briefly how members of all races in our society may reach their dreams.

- Are there any special obstacles that minorities might encounter? What are they?

Creating Images

Imagery is a form of figurative language that creates mental images (pictures). John Steinbeck uses imagery in *The Pearl* to help create pictures with words. One example of imagery occurs when the family and town head out to see the doctor.

> *"They made a quick soft-footed procession into the center of the town, first Juana and Kino, and behind them Juan Tomás and Apolonia and her big stomach jiggling with the strenuous pace, then all the neighbors with the children trotting on the flanks. And the yellow sun threw their black shadows ahead of them so that they walked on their own shadows."*

Your Turn:

After locating examples of imagery for each of the people and places below, work with a partner to create a drawing of the mental image the author has created for you. Use crayons, colored pencils, or markers to add color.

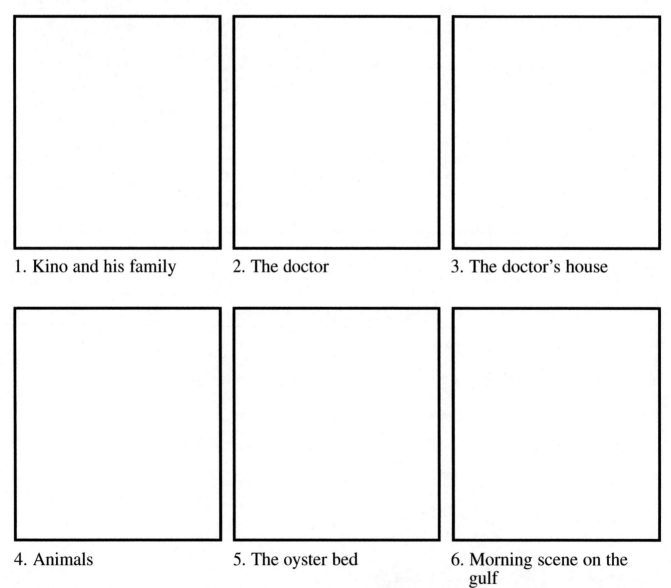

1. Kino and his family

2. The doctor

3. The doctor's house

4. Animals

5. The oyster bed

6. Morning scene on the gulf

Science: Poison

In *The Pearl*, baby Coyotito is stung by a scorpion. A scorpion is a small animal with a dangerous sting. Many animals use poison as a way to protect themselves. Some examples include the Gila monster lizard, the death puffer fish, the arrow poison frog, the king cobra snake, and the black widow spider.

However, animals are not the only ones who have poisons. Several types of household cleaning products are poisonous if used incorrectly. Many plants are poisonous. Drugs can also be poisonous if directions aren't followed exactly.

There are many reasons poison is so dangerous. Some poisons may be harmful to one type of animal but not another. Do some research about poisons. Then use the information to fill out the chart below.

Poison	Sources of Poison	Symptoms	Antidotes

Reading Response Journals

One great way to insure that the reading of *The Pearl* touches each student in a personal way is to include the use of Reading Response Journals in your plans. In these journals, students can be encouraged to respond to the story in a number of ways. Here are a few ideas.

- Tell students that the purpose of the journal is to record their thoughts, ideas, observations, and questions as they read *The Pearl*.

- Provide students with, or ask them to suggest, topics from the story that would stimulate writing. Here are a few examples from the chapters in Section 1.

     — Kino is just one of many of his village's pearl divers. Describe some of the dangers these divers face.

     — What are some dangerous occupations in our area that you might consider as careers?

     — How is the role that Juana played in *The Pearl* different from the women you know?

- After the reading of each chapter, students can write one or more new things they learned in the chapter.

- Ask students to draw their responses to certain events or characters in the story, using blank pages in their journals.

- Tell students that they may use their journals to record "diary-type" responses that they may want to enter.

- Encourage students to bring their journal ideas to life! Ideas generated from their journal writing can be used to create plays, debates, stories, songs, and art displays.

Allow students time to write in their journals daily. To evaluate the journals, you may wish to use the following guidelines.

- Personal reflections will be read by the teacher, but no corrections or letter grades will be assigned. Credit is given for effort, and all students who sincerely try will be awarded credit. If a grade is desired for this type of entry, grade according to the of journal entries completed. For example, if five journal assignments were made and the student conscientiously completes all five, then he or she should receive an "A."

- Nonjudgmental teacher responses should be made as you read the journals to let the students know that you are reading and enjoying their journals. Here are some types of responses that will please your journal writers and encourage them to write more.

     — "You have really found what's important in the story!"

     — "You've made me feel as if I'm there."

     — "If you feel comfortable, I'd like for you to share this with the class. I think they'll enjoy it as much as I have."

Quiz

1. On the back of this page, write a paragraph summarizing Chapter III. Then complete the rest of the questions on this page.

2. To what does the author compare the news traveling through the town?

   _____

   _____

3. Why does the priest wonder "whether he had baptized Kino's baby" or married him?

   _____

   _____

4. What was the author's purpose for having the doctor see himself "sitting in a restaurant in Paris," after hearing of The Pearl of the World?

   _____

   _____

5. How did Kino become "everyone's enemy"?

   _____

   _____

6. What did Kino want for himself that showed that he, too, was infected with the poison of greed?

   _____

   _____

7. How were the priest and the doctor similar in their treatment of Kino?

   _____

   _____

8. What foreshadowing event helps to show the priest's greedy interests in the pearl?

   _____

   _____

9. Where did Kino finally hide his pearl?

   _____

   _____

10. What was Juana's opinion of this great pearl?

    _____

    _____

Characterization

Characterization is an author's way of explaining the people in a story. It is the technique an author uses to add color or depth to his characters. Working like an artist at a canvas, the author first sketches his character lightly. This allows the reader to become involved. As the story unfolds, the author adds a stroke of color here and a highlight there, helping to make the character become more clearly focused. By the end of the story, there will be no doubt as to the qualities and weaknesses of his characters.

For example, here is how the character of Juana is developed:

Juana: The first thing upon awakening "she went to the hanging box where Coyotito slept, and leaned over it and said a little reassuring word."

Characteristic: a loving and devoted mother

Juana: When told that the doctor would not help her son, the author adds more to her character. Juana looked up, "her eyes as cold as the eyes of a lioness."

Characteristic: protective, strong as a lion; deadly

Your Turn:

Individually or in small groups find similar examples of characterization from the book for the characters below. Copy the quote and tell what characteristic is expressed. Do two of your own.

Kino: _____

_____

Characteristic: _____

_____

Doctor: _____

_____

Characteristic: _____

_____: _____

Priest: _____

_____

Characteristic: _____

_____: _____

Characterization Teams

A character is generally developed in four ways.

1. way is when the author tells us.

   Example: "Kino felt weak and afraid and angry."

2. Another way is by writing how a character acts.

   Example: When the doctor discovered where Kino hid his pearl, Kino wisely waits until the doctor leaves. Then, he dug another hole in the dirt floor so no one would find it. This act shows that he was a wise man.

3. A third way is by a character's thoughts or words.

   Example: Kino says that because of the pearl Juana will have a new shawl and skirt while Coyotito will go to school. This indicates that Kino is a good man and loves his family.

4. The final way is by the reactions of others.

   Example: When Kino found the great pearl, men said of him that his eyes shone and that he had become "a great man." From those words you can tell that people thought well of him.

You Try It

In a group of three or more, interview each group member to find out about his/her interests, hobbies, families, likes and dislikes. Listen carefully. Then, as a group, write about each person, utilizing each of the characterization techniques listed above.

   Example: Chris is happy. (example 1—happy) "Next week is my birthday," she announced, eagerly. (example 3—excited) She tapped her pencil against her leg, (example 2—nervous) as the group laughed at her vivid description of her little brother. (example 4—funny)

Exchange these with your classmates orally and have them identify the types of characterization used.

Marine Biology

Under Kino's quiet lagoon in the gulf, life was much different than life in the little fishing village. Certainly, the sea creatures must have been of interest to Kino and his fellow fishermen, as life below the surface of the mirror-like water was a strange and sometimes dangerous new world. One item of particular interest to them, of course, would be the oyster and the treasure-that-might-be, the pearl.

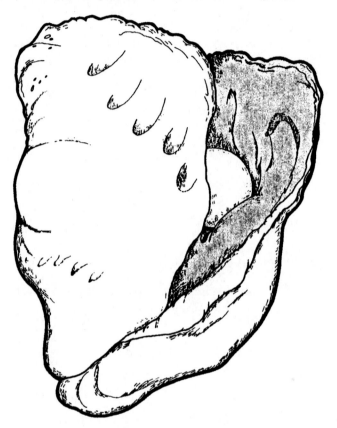

Oyster

Oysters are bivalved (two-shelled) mollusks that live in the sea. They produce a smooth lining inside their shells that is often lustrous. When a grain of sand or other foreign object invades the oyster, the cells which line the inside of the shell surround the grain of sand. Layer upon layer of these cells cover this, forming a pearl. Pearls are considered one of the most valuable of all gems. They are soft, and absorb as well as reflect light.

There must have been many other interesting creatures in Kino's second world under the lagoon. A few possibilities are listed below. Using reference books, look them up and report on their special characteristics as in the example above. Illustrate. Assemble into a class book.

- Lobster

- Killer Whale

- Turtle

- Great White Shark

- Manta Ray

Add any others that you find interesting and share with the class.

There Ought to Be a Law

We only have to turn on the television set or open the newspaper to find out the problems that exist in our society. It might seem strange to you that even in Kino's tiny world of La Paz, there were problems as well. Some of the problems that Kino has experienced would have solutions if he were in the United States at the present time.

For example, what would happen to you if you were taken to the hospital for an emergency such as Coyotito had and the doctor refused to see you, hinting that you were just an animal? What legal steps could your parents take if the hospital wouldn't help you and let you die because you were poor or the "wrong" race?

As a class, brainstorm a list of what might be done if Kino had had this experience in the present day United States rather than in La Paz.

Using the brainstormed list, choose the solution that you feel most strongly about. Now pretend that you are a newsperson. Use the information from the brainstorming to write an article explaining the outrageous and humiliating experience this family and their community has just undergone.

As in any good news article, include the five W's. Use the outline to help you organize your information.

Who: _____

_____

What:_____

_____

When: _____

_____

Where:_____

_____

Why: _____

_____

After proofreading your article, exchange it with a partner. Have your partner create an eye-catching headline. Share these with the class.

Quiz

1. On the back of this paper, write a one paragraph summary of the major events in Chapter IV. Then complete the rest of the questions on this page.

2. Who knew that Kino was going to sell his pearl?

   _____

   _____

3. Describe the "arrangement" the pearl sellers had made between themselves in order to cheat Kino.

   _____

   _____

4. What was the one thing the pearl buyers were reluctant to do?

   _____

   _____

5. What happened to the men before Kino when they traveled to the capital to sell their pearls?

   _____

   _____

6. Why did the pearl buyer say that Kino's pearl was just "fool's gold"?

   _____

   _____

7. Although Kino was offered 1500 pesos, he did not sell it. Why did many of Kino's townspeople think it was a fair offer?

   _____

   _____

8. Even though he is afraid, Kino is determined. What does he decide to do?

   _____

   _____

9. What replaced The Song of the Family after the meeting with the pearl dealers?

   _____

   _____

10. What happens to Kino that night?

   _____

   _____

A Dream Come True

As you have read, all of Kino's dreams are wrapped up in his Pearl of the World. He has seen visions of a new life within the pearl's beautiful "incandescence." He sees new clothes for his wife. He sees himself in "new white clothes" with a hat, "not a straw hat" either. His son wears a little sailor suit "from the United States." All these are things he wants. In essence, he wants a better life for himself and his family. Near the beginning of Chapter IV, Kino's neighbors speak of what they would do if they had found the pearl and how they hope it will not destroy Kino.

Suppose you came into sudden great fortune by inheriting some money, winning a contest, or finding something of great value that you were allowed to keep. Answer the questions below to make a plan for using your new-found wealth.

- How much money would you like to have? (Be realistic!)

- What are some things you would like to have for yourself, and how much does each cost?

- What are some things you would like to have for your family, and how much does each cost?

- What are your favorite charities, and how much money or what items would you like to donate to each?

- Would you save or invest some of the money? Where would you put it? Why?

- How would you change if you had this money? Would your personality be different?

- How do you think people would treat you? Is that different from the way you are treated now?

Write a budget for your new-found wealth and present it to a small group of your classmates. Listen to their reactions and suggestions. Then, finalize your plan.

Writing Corner

Since we have seen the "poison-sacs" of the town swell with the black bile of greed and even murder, it's an easy guess that things are a bit grim for Kino. The conspiracy of the pearl buyers has driven Kino to desperate action. He is determined to go to the capital to sell his ticket out of poverty—the pearl.

Suppose the publisher of this book had had enough of this depressing slant to the novel. What if he sent the manuscript back to Mr. Steinbeck and told him to rewrite that chapter, with the pearl buyers being honest and helpful to Kino.

Mr. Steinbeck found it objectionable and refused to do this. In a rage, he discarded the whole project and threw it out the window. Suppose further that one of your friends found it, and you all decided you could finish it yourself with a happier conclusion to the sale of the pearl.

You Write It!

You and your "friends" (group) are to change what happened in the pearl-buying sequence. Your writing should reflect the same style as the author. It needs to include dialogue, description of the room, and the actions of the characters involved. Start when Kino enters the room with the pearl buyer who was described as a "jolly man who knew all the jokes" whose "eyes twinkled with friendship."

Don't forget, you'll be paid well. So do a good job.

Dollar Exchange

The type of money or currency used in one country is not necessarily the same as that used in another. The worth of United States currency is called the Dollar Exchange Rate. A table listing countries, the name of their currency, and rates of exchange appear daily in many newspapers.

Find a Dollar Exchange Rate Table in the newspaper. Look at it. What is the rate of exchange for the Mexican peso, the Canadian dollar, the Belgian franc? To determine how much money is worth use this formula: $U.S. x Foreign Exchange Rate= Total in Foreign Currency.

Dollars = Pesos

To complete this assignment you will need a current Dollar Exchange Rate Table from the newspaper. Use it to determine the exchange rate of the Mexican peso.

Now pretend you arrive for a vacation in Mexico with 5,000 U.S. dollars. You need to visit a money exchange center. How many pesos will you have? (Your answer will vary depending on the exchange rate you use.)

First, make a list of things you will need. These should include lodging, food, and transportation. You may also want to include equipment such as a snorkel, surfboard, and special vacation clothing like swimwear and evening clothes.

Using sources, such as catalogs, ads in magazines, travel brochures, and newspapers, write down the costs and convert them to pesos. Keep a running total of pesos and subtract it from your total amount of pesos. What will your vacation money buy?

Use the chart below to help keep track of the items you need to buy, the cost in both dollars and pesos, and a running total of how much you have spent.

Item	Cost in Dollars	Cost in Pesos

The "Right" Look

We are a curious species. Universally, it is essential to dress a certain way. We expect this. In school, students dress the way their particular group expects them to. They may wear what professional athletes do. Perhaps the latest rock star will be the model for the new "in" look. Sometimes the way people dress is like wearing a new costume.

This was true for Kino as well. The author describes how Kino dressed for his big day of the pearl sale:

> *"Kino put on his large hat and felt it with his hand to see that it was properly placed, not on the back or side of his head, like a rash, unmarried, irresponsible man, and not flat as an elder would wear it, but tilted a little forward to show aggressiveness and seriousness and vigor."*

Here we see Kino playing the role of a man about to engage in serious business, therefore he assumed the "right" look. What "costumes" would be appropriate for people with the following occupations or hobbies? Write and illustrate a description of what their clothes would look like. Give the reasons you feel your choice of clothing is appropriate.

- Banker
- Jogger
- Golfer
- Librarian
- Fast Food Attendant
- Welder
- Farmer
- TV Newsperson
    a. Anchorman
    b. Weatherman
    c. War Corespondent
    d. Fashion Expert
- Teacher
- Author
- Pilot
- Others of your choice

Quiz

1. On the back of this paper, write a one paragraph summary of the events that took place in Chapter V. Then, complete the questions on the rest of this page.

2. What did Juana try to do with which Kino strongly disagreed?

   _____

   _____

3. What type of action did Kino take to prevent this?

   _____

   _____

4. Discuss the event that took place after he recovered his prized pearl.

   _____

   _____

5. Although Kino reminds Juana several times that he is a "man," Juana knows that she is a "woman." What quality of being a woman does she rely on to "save them all"?

   _____

   _____

6. After Kino ordered Juana to return to their house, what, to her surprise, did she find?

   _____

   _____

7. What did Kino's brother do for them after that?

   _____

   _____

8. Why was the damage to Kino's boat so devastating?

   _____

   _____

9. Discuss the danger it was for Juan Tomas to hide Kino's family.

   _____

   _____

10. Which direction would Kino take to escape the village?

   _____

   _____

Investigative Reporter

In this exercise you are a big city reporter. You were originally on a charter fishing trip and recently moored your vessel in the peaceful harbor of La Paz. You were on the docks the day of Kino's great discovery and have followed the turn of events with a keen interest. After this latest tragedy, you called your office in Mazatlan for permission to investigate this bizarre case.

Your task here is to ask the following questions and to record what Kino's responses are, in an attempt to unearth the truth.

Reporter: Well, Kino, when did the pearl and its possession first seem to be a problem for you?

Kino: _____

_____

Reporter: What specific thing made you aware that it was a source of danger?

Kino: _____

_____

Reporter: You spoke earlier of "The Song of Evil." Who brought the song to you?

Kino: _____

_____

Reporter: Who was present when you heard these evil forewarnings of danger?

Kino: _____

_____

Reporter: Please search your mind. Who do you suspect, or who has shown an unusual interest in you lately?

Kino: _____

_____

Reporter: Just what unusual interest have they displayed? For instance, do you suspect the pearl buyers?

Kino: _____

_____

Reporter: You mentioned also the doctor might have poisoned Coyotito. Would you explain any possible motive that he might have had to inflict pain on your baby?

Kino: _____

_____

As a reporter you should now summarize your findings, and reach an objective conclusion as to what should be done to right all the wrongs done to Kino.

Sherlock Holmes

Kino and his family have been zeroed in on from many sides. The beggars want it, the shopkeepers want it, the doctor lusts after it, the unknown man behind the pearl buyers wants it, and even the priest is determined to get it. The "it" in this case is the pearl and the money it represents. Three times, unknown people referred to as shadowy "dark" figures have attacked them. They finally destroy Kino's home and expose the family to the ultimate danger, death.

Attempted Murder Theory

Working with a partner, create your own theory as to who is responsible. For example, do you think the doctor hired some thugs to steal the pearl or murder Kino to obtain it? Could it be one of his jealous pearl diving friends?

Use the lines below and on the back of this paper to write up your theory about who the culprits are. Use the style of Sherlock Holmes or any other detective familiar to you.

Your theory should include the following:

- Who is doing this?
- What are their motives?
- How are they going about it so as not to be detected?

Your thieves should also be overheard in a conversation plotting how they are going to get the pearl on their next attempt.

_____

_____

_____

_____

_____

_____

_____

_____

_____

When you are finished, share your theories with the class and vote on which seems the most believable.

Geography

The Pearl takes place in La Paz, Mexico which, according to the story, is a village located on a beach on the Gulf of California.

Use an atlas or similar reference book to familiarize yourself with Kino's geographical area. Then, draw a map of the area. Chart the escape route which Kino and his family will take. He needs to find a large city in which to conclude his business. You decide where he can go. Include a key on your map. Name significant features on your map using symbols of your own choice. After your map and escape route are completed and colored, write an accompanying journal entry from Kino's point of view of his escape and the hardships endured.

Problem Solving

Throughout this section, Kino is bombarded with problems.

The first is when his own wife, Juana, attempted to steal his ticket to great wealth and a better life, his pearl. His reaction is strong. We are told that a great "rage surged in Kino." As he searched for her, "his brain was red with anger." Finally he caught her and solved the problem. "He struck her in her face with his clenched fist" knocked her to the ground and "kicked her." He "hissed at her like a snake" and looked at her with murder in his heart.

He did solve his problem, but his method was quite primitive.

Alternatives

On the next few lines, rewrite that section. Begin with Kino waking up to discover Juana and the pearl missing. Unlike Kino, you are to use your brain and cool, uncluttered logic to retrieve both Juana and the pearl.

_____

_____

_____

_____

_____

_____

Think of 3 problems that you have had in the past and write how you solved them in an intelligent manner. On the back of this paper, write down one that you had that you might have handled differently now that you are older.

Problem 1: _____

Solution: _____

Problem 2: _____

Solution: _____

Problem 3: _____

Solution: _____

Quiz

1. On the back of this paper, write a one page paragraph summarizing the major events in Chapter VI. Then complete the rest of the questions on this page.

2. What was the mood and setting like when Kino's family exited the town?

   _____

   _____

3. How did this reinforce or make the story better?

   _____

   _____

4. What time of day did they leave town?

   _____

   _____

5. What clever thing did Kino do to try to fool anyone that might be tracking them?

   _____

   _____

6. What convinces Kino that the pearl was not valueless as Juana suggested to him?

   _____

   _____

7. When or what did Kino discover that told him that his escape might not be so easy?

   _____

   _____

8. What did Kino see "gleaming in the sun" that one of the trackers had in his hand?

   _____

   _____

9. What happens to Coyotito at the little water pool in the high desert?

   _____

   _____

10. What did Kino finally do with his priceless pearl?

    _____

    _____

Personification

Throughout this book you have been introduced to a variety of literary techniques which the author has used to great effect in his novel, *The Pearl*. Personification is one of those techniques.

Personification is giving human characteristics to something that is not human. John Steinbeck writes that, "The wind blew fierce and strong, and it pelted them with bits of sticks, sand, and little rocks." Here, the suggestion is that the wind has the human ability to be "strong" and is able to pelt or throw "sticks, sand, and little rocks" at Juana, Kino, and Coyotito.

Another example, from the same page goes on to say "The sky was brushed clean by the wind and the stars were cold in the black sky." The wind in this case gives us the picture of having a brush and cleaning up the sky. Also, it is not stars but people who are "cold."

The author uses the technique of personification throughout this book to show that Kino and his family, as well as the environment, are all alive in his story. Each element is related equally to the other.

Your task is to explain the human qualities that the following examples of personification show us. Write out what each example means.

Example 1: "The wind cried and whisked in the brush, and the family went on monotonously, hour after hour."

_____

_____

Example 2: "High in the gray stone mountains, under a frowning peak, a little spring bubbled . . ."

_____

_____

Example 3: "There wasn't much left of it then anyway, for every time it fell over an escarpment the thirsty air drank it . . ."

_____

_____

Example 4: "The coyotes cried and laughed in the brush."

_____

_____

Example 5: "The high sun streamed down on the dry creaking earth so that the vegetation ticked in protest."

_____

_____

Personification Artists

In this exercise you and your partner will use the skills which you practiced on page 31 to explain the technique of personification.

Skim the book and locate examples of personification. At the bottom of the boxes below write examples that you find. Use quotation marks and copy the words very carefully. Highlight the human quality that is being showcased. Exchange papers with your partner. In the boxes, your partner will draw a literal interpretation of the quotation, for example, a frowning mountain.

Example 1

Example 2

Example 3

Example 4

Science: The Desert

Kino and his family ventured basically into the unknown on their trek. They never encountered such harsh terrain and hostile weather as they had in this desert area in which they found themselves.

In this lesson, you will be consulting the text itself and appropriate resource books. In the boxes below write down natural features and plants that the author tells you that are part of the environment and list animals found there.

Next, use resource materials and write down other information about the environment and unique vegetation found in this area of Mexico. Also, list the animals typical to this harsh region. Compare what you find in *The Pearl* to what you find in resources.

Environment	Environment
The Pearl	**The Pearl**
Resources	**Resources**

Survival

Kino and his family were on the run and were being hunted like animals. Along with that, they had to deal with the "cricking heat" of the desert. The author does not go into much detail about how they survived other than to mention a few gourds of water and corncakes. Kino did not know how far he had to go or what direction to travel in order to reach the capital.

Creative Writing

You are to take the same journey as Kino. However, you will have the advantage of knowing what the environment is like. (See Science, page 33.) Take into account the information you have accumulated. Make a list of items that you will need in order to survive this ordeal. Remember, you will be carrying the items, so limit yourself to no more than ten you can carry. Think carefully as you plan your journey. Once you have left, there is no turning back.

You will not have the trackers after you, only the relentless beating of the sun and lack of water. List the items you plan to take below.

_____   _____

_____   _____

_____   _____

_____   _____

_____   _____

Use the lines below to write a paragraph discussing the obstacles you will face and how you will be prepared to overcome each.

_____

_____

_____

_____

_____

_____

_____

_____

_____

Any Questions?

When you finished reading *The Pearl,* did you have some questions that were left unanswered? Write them here.

_____

_____

_____

Then work in groups or by yourself to prepare possible answers for the questions you have asked above or some of those written below. When you have finished, share your ideas with the class.

- What do you think happened to Kino and Juana after they returned to their village?

- What do you think would have happened if Kino had not given his triumphant shout after he had found the pearl?

- Would he have been able to successfully sell his pearl somewhere if he kept it a secret?

- Why do you think the author bothered to have all that information about Coyotito being stung by the scorpion?

- How would the story have been changed if the priest was more helpful to Kino, and not filled with greed as the doctor was?

- Why did the author tell us that Kino went beyond all boundaries when he wanted a steel harpoon and a rifle?

- What do you think Kino would have done if Juana had accomplished her goal in destroying the pearl when she originally stole it and ran into the night?

- Why was it important to the story that their house was burned to the ground?

- How did the contrast in living conditions between those of the walled city and Kino's village help the story?

- What do you think the doctor would have done if he had been able to obtain the pearl from Kino? What evidence from the story leads you to think this might have happened?

- Do you think it might have been one of the greedy pearl buyers who was after the pearl? If so, how do you think he could overturn things and become the top man?

- Do you think the beggars were capable of mounting this assault on Kino and his family?

- Why do you think Kino did not just borrow his brother's canoe? Is there any evidence from the book that supports your thinking?

- Would the outcome of the story have been any different if Kino and his family had been able to get the use of a canoe?

- Why do you think it was necessary for the author to have Coyotito shot and killed?

- Why would Kino and Juana return to their village with their dead son?

- Do you think they could just "start all over" in their village?

- Why did the author not have Juana walking behind Kino on their return to the village as was normal?

Book Report Ideas

There are numerous ways to report on a book once you have read it. After you have finished reading *The Pearl*, choose one method of reporting on the book that interests you. It may be a way that your teacher suggests, an idea of your own, or one of the ways that is mentioned below.

- **See What I Read?**
  This report is a visual one. A model of a scene from the story can be created, or a likeness of one or more of the characters from the story can be drawn or sculpted.

- **Time Capsule**
  This report provides people living at a future time with the reasons *The Pearl* is such an outstanding book and gives these future people reasons why it should be read. Make a "time capsule" and neatly print or write your reasons inside the capsule. You may wish to "bury" your capsule after you have shared it with your classmates. Perhaps one day someone will find it and read *The Pearl* because of what you wrote!

- **Come To Life!**
  This report is one that lends itself to a group project. A size-appropriate group prepares a scene from the story for dramatization, acts it out, and relates the significance of the scene to the entire book. Costumes and props will add to the dramatization!

- **Into the Future**
  This report predicts what might happen if *The Pearl* were to continue. It may take the form of a story in narrative or dramatic form, or a visual display.

- **Guess Who or What**
  This report is similar to "Twenty Questions." The reporter gives a series of clues about a character from the story in a vague to precise, general to specific order. After all clues have been given, the identity of the mystery character must be deduced. After the character has been guessed, the same reporter presents another "Twenty Clues" about an event in the story.

- **A Character Comes To Life!**
  Suppose one of the characters in *The Pearl* came to life and walked into your home or classroom. This report gives a view of what this character sees, hears, and feels as he or she experiences the world in which you live.

- **Sales Talk**
  This report serves as an advertisement to "sell" *The Pearl* to one or more specific groups. You decide on the group to target and the sales pitch you will use. Include some kind of graphics in your presentation.

- **Coming Attraction!**
  The Pearl is about to be made into a movie, and you have been chosen to design the promotional poster. Include the title and author of the book, a listing of the main characters and the contemporary actors who will play them, a drawing of a scene from the book, and a paragraph synopsis of the story.

- **Literary Interview**
  This report is done in pairs. One student will pretend to be a character in the story, steeped completely in the persona of his or her character. The other student will play the role of a television or radio interviewer, trying to provide the audience with insights into the character's personality and life. It is the responsibility of the partners to create meaningful questions and appropriate responses.

La Paz Revisited

You are the same reporter who interviewed Kino while you were in the harbor fifteen years ago. (See page 26.) Now retired, you are devoting your time to your favorite hobby, sport-fishing. Out of curiosity, you wonder what happened to Kino and the "under-society,' of the pearl fishermen. Some of the questions you have are:

—Have living conditions changed for the village people?
—Are Kino and his family still there?
—Did little Coyotito survive his scorpion sting?

You Try It: Make a list of 10 questions for Kino and his townspeople to answer. After you complete this list, give it to your partner to answer. Meanwhile, answer your partner's questions. Share some questions and replies with the class.

1. Question: _____
   Reply: _____

2. Question: _____
   Reply: _____

3. Question: _____
   Reply: _____

4. Question: _____
   Reply: _____

5. Question: _____
   Reply: _____

6. Question: _____
   Reply: _____

7. Question: _____
   Reply: _____

8. Question: _____
   Reply: _____

9. Question: _____
   Reply: _____

10. Question: _____
    Reply: _____

The Essay

Throughout this unit you have looked at, studied and had "hands-on" experience with some of the literary techniques used by John Steinbeck in his timeless novel, *The Pearl*. Specifically, characterization, imagery, foreshadowing, and personification were studied. In some instances you had to explain the examples provided, and in others you had to provide examples yourselves.

You will now be given the opportunity to demonstrate a working knowledge of these techniques. You will be required to demonstrate your knowledge by pointing them out as you develop your essay.

Themes

You are to discuss the themes of greed and prejudice in *The Pearl*. You will need an introductory paragraph with an effective "lead-in." This paragraph will also be where you state your purpose (what you are going to prove) and how you will go about it.

As you develop your paper, show how the use of literary techniques by John Steinbeck help to add depth and clarity to his work. An example of this is the characterization of the doctor. This is so clearly accomplished, we automatically side with the oppressed Kino.

Since you have two themes, develop each one separately. For example, start with the prejudice theme and develop it thoroughly before starting with the one concerned with greed or avarice, symbolically referred to as a poison by Steinbeck. (The greed theme is more prevalent in the story and more time should be spent developing it.)

Remember to support your ideas with facts from the book. Also, when appropriate, show how some of Steinbeck's literary skills reinforce or add depth to his writing. Use the following ideas to help organize your thoughts and for your rough draft. Attach them to your final copy.

Ways to Organize Your Thoughts

In writing the essay, it will be helpful to spend time organizing your thoughts. There are many techniques to help you to do this.

Venn Diagram

A Venn diagram is a comparison chart. It is usually two circles overlapping. Both outer circles list the characteristic unique to each of the subjects. The overlapping circles list the characteristics in common. Information from brainstorming can be transferred into the diagram, and paragraphs can come from that.

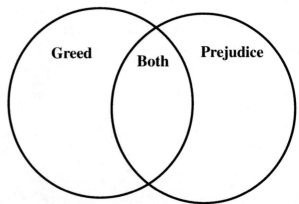

The Essay (cont.)

The Outline

The most traditional organizational tool is the outline. There are two types of outlines. One is a topic outline which lists topics or ideas to be covered. Since you don't use sentences, this works well for a short paper. A more detailed sentence outline contains major points and many supporting details. The outline format for both types is:

I. Greed

    A. _____

    B. _____

        1. _____

        2. _____

            a. _____

            b. _____

                (1) _____

                (2) _____

II. Prejudice

Remember that in outlining for every 1 you must have a 2; each "a" must have a "b."

Story Cluster or Web

For this type of organization, you choose a topic, such as "greed," and place it in a circle in the center of a page. As ideas about the topic that pertain to the story come to you, jot them down. Since this is for organization purposes, you can write down anything and then use only what is appropriate to your essay.

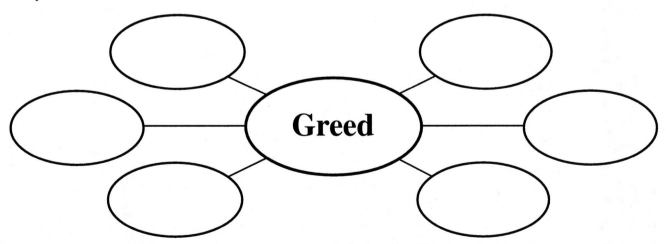

After you have done some organizing, it is time to write your essay.

Use pages 38–40 to organize and write a rough draft.

The Essay *(cont.)*

Use this page to help write a rough draft. When you have finished your rough draft, spend some time polishing and revising it. Correct grammar, usage, spelling, and mechanics. Copy it over, and turn in a final copy along with a rough draft.

Topic or opening paragraph—State the purpose of your essay.

Developmental paragraphs—This is the main idea or body of your essay. Start with either theme, prejudice or greed, and develop it. Write a separate paragraph(s) for each. Give three examples or proof for each topic. (Use your outline, Venn diagram, or clusters to help with this.) These can be incidents or specific quotes from the novel. If you use quotes, be sure to copy them exactly as they are in the book and use quotation marks. Explain your proof. Tell why your examples show prejudice or greed.

Closing paragraph—Here is where you tie your entire essay together. Summarize your points on prejudice and greed and draw a conclusion.

Use this paragraph outline as a model. You may need to use several sheets of paper to write your essay.

Title

Topic Paragraph

Developmental Paragraph(s)

Closing Paragraph

Design a Book Cover

An important element to every literary work is the work done by the publisher's artists. Along with doing timely illustrations throughout the book, it is most important to develop an eye-catching book cover. This cover should spark the imagination of the prospective reader. It needs to include the book title, the author's name, and a scene or information that is in the book. Create an imaginative, artistic, and eye-catching book cover for *The Pearl*. Use your knowledge of the book to create the cover.

Unit Test

Matching: Match the quotes with the people who said them.

> doctor   Juana   Kino   pries   pearl buyer

1. _____ " 'You have heard of fool's gold. It is too large. It is a curiosity only.' "

2. _____ " 'This thing is evil. This pearl is a sin. It will destroy us.' "

3. _____ " 'Do you keep the pearl in a safe place? Perhaps you would like me to put it in my safe? It would be a shame to have it stolen before you could sell it.' "

4. _____ " 'Thou art named after a great man. Thy namesake tamed the desert. It is in the books.' "

5. _____ " 'Our son must go to school. He must break out of the pot that holds us in.' "

True or False: Write true or false next to each statement below.

1. _____ The pearl buyers offered Kino a fair price, considering the pearl was a curiosity only.

2. _____ The priest was a good man who had Kino's interests at heart.

3. _____ Juana was a weak and timid person.

4. _____ Juana and Kino are wiser at the end of the story.

5. _____ Kino never understood the evil of the pearl.

Short Answer: Provide a short answer for each of these questions.

1. What does Juana do that shows her strength in Chapter 1?

   _____

2. Why is the crowd shamed when the doctor's servant tells Kino, "The doctor has gone out"?

   _____

3. When Kino and Juana returned to their village, why did the villagers draw back?

   _____

4. Why did the pearl look gray and ulcerous at the end of the story?

   _____

5. Why did Juana let Kino throw the pearl away after he offered to let her do it?

   _____

Essay: Write these essays on the back of this paper.

1. Discuss how the pearl poisoned the little town of La Paz.

2. Juana once said that Kino was "a man, half insane and half god." Explain what she might have meant.

Response

Explain the meaning of each of these quotations from *The Pearl*.

Chapter I: " 'Have I nothing better to do than to cure insect bitesfor "little Indians "? I am a doctor, not a veterinary'."

Chapter I: *"For a long time Kino stood in front of the gate with Juana beside him. Slowly he put his suppliant hat on his head. Then without warning, he struck the gate a crushing blow with his fist."*

Chapter II: *"But in the song there was a secret little inner song, hardly perceptible, but always there, sweet and secret and clinging, almost hiding in the counter-melody and this was the Song of the Pearl That Might Be."*

Chapter II: *"And to Kino the secret melody of the maybe pearl broke clear and beautiful, rich and warm and lovely, glowing and gloating and triumphant."*

Chapter II: *"His emotions broke over him. He put back his head and howled. His eyes rolled up and he screamed and his body went rigid."*

Chapter III: *"The news . . . came to the priest walking in his garden, and it put a thoughtful look in his eyes and a memory of certain repairs necessary to the church."*

Chapter III: *"The news came to the shopkeepers and they looked at the men's clothes that had not sold as well."*

Chapter III: *"The doctor looked past his aged patient and saw himself sitting in a restaurant in Paris and a waiter was just opening a bottle of wine."*

Chapter III: *". . . Kino's pearl went into the dreams, the speculations, the schemes, the plans, the futures, the wishes, the needs, the lusts, the hungers, of everyone, and only one person stood in the way and that was Kino so that he became curiously every man's enemy."*

Chapter IV: *After Kinofinally put the pearl on the velvet tray, ". . . the secret hand behind the desk missed in its precision. The coin stumbled over a knuckle and slipped silently into the dealer's lap."*

Chapter IV: *Kino's neighbors "had been afraid of something like this. The pearl was large, but it had a strange color. They had been suspicious of itirom thefirst. And after all, a thousand pesos was not to be thrown away. It was comparative wealth to a man who was not wealthy. Only yesterday Kino had nothing."*

Chapter V: *"Juana knew that the old life was goneforever. A dead man in the path, and Kino's knife, dark bladed beside him, convinced her."*

Chapter VI: *"The sun was behind them and their long shadows stalked ahead and they seemed to carry two towers of darkness with them."*

Teacher Note: Choose an appropriate number of quotes for your students.

Conversations

Work in size-appropriate groups to write and perform the conversations that might have occurred in each of the following situations.

- Kino goes to the priest to ask him to see if he could get the doctor to attend Coyotito. (3 people)

- Juan Tomas and the fishermen meet to think of a way to get the doctor to help Kino. (5 people)

- The beggars talk together about the chances of Kino getting help from the doctor. The conversation should include the doctor's abilities, greed, sins, and appetites. (4 people)

- Kino excitedly returns from his dive, scrambles aboard his canoe and reveals his excitement to Juana. She replies, and they discuss their possible future. (2 people)

- The crews of various boats converse when they hear Kino's triumphant scream. (3 boats, 6 people)

- Various groups in the town perform the operation of informing the whole town "faster than small boys can scramble and dart to tell it." (entire class)

- The doctor converses with his patient as he hears of the news. (2 people)

- The priest hears the news in his garden from his housekeeper. (2 people)

- The beggars hear and discuss the news while standing by the church on the town's square. (6 people)

- The pearl buyers meet with their head buyer as he outlines his plans to get a good deal on this pearl. (6people)

- Juan Tomas and Apolonia discuss what will happen to Kino's life now that he is "rich." (2 people)

- A group of pearl divers discuss the great luck of Kino and determine to return to Kino's spot on the gulf the next day. (6 people)

- The pearl thieves meet after wounding Kino and failing to get the Pearl of the World. Are they arguing among themselves or making further, more ruthless plans? (3 people)

- The Chinese grocery-store owners discuss how much money Kino might get today from the pearl buyers and their plan on getting their "share" as well. (3 people)

- Various neighbors weigh Kino's chances to strike it rich and have a good chance at a new life. Included will be a discussion on how Kino could be helpful to each of them in return. (Two groups of 4 fishermen)

- The pearl salesmen meet with the head pearl salesman after they have outraged Kino and did not make the deal that they planned to make. (6 people)

- After discovering the ruined canoe, Kino, Juana and Juan Tomas discuss his options of getting to safety.

- Worried neighbors discuss how Kino is making their lives dangerous by his behavior. (4 people)

- After Kino kills the robber and Kino's house gets torched, the pearl fishermen meet to decide to tell Kino that he must leave for the good of the village or meet the price that the pearl buyers set. (5 people)

- Townspeople discuss Kino's sudden disappearance. Come up with three different theories as to where he went or what happened to him. (3 people)

- The three trackers talk the first night about what their plan will be when they catch Kino. (3 people)

- Kino and Juana converse after killing the trackers and try to decide when and where to bury Coyotito. Why did they decide to return to La Paz? (2 people)

Bibliography

Fiction

Aiken, Joan. *Dido and Pa* (Delacourt, 1986)

Aiken, Joan. *The Wolves of Willingby Chase* (Dell, 1987)

Bawden, Mna. *Devil by the Sea* (Harper, 1976)

Brandel, Marc. *The Mystery of the Two-Toed Pigeon* (Random, 1984)

Christian, Mary Blount. *Man in Catfish Bay* (Whitman, 1985)

Cross, Gillian. *On the Edge* (Holiday, 1985)

Defoe, Daniel. *Robinson Crusoe* (Putnam, 1963)

Fleischman, Paul. *The Half Moon Inn* (Harper, 1980)

George, Jean Craighead. *Julie of the Wolves* (Harper, 1972)

George, Jean Craighead. *My Side of the Mountain* (Dutton, 1959)

George, Jean Craighead. *Shark Beneath the Reef* (Harper, 1989)

Gray, Patsey. *Barefoot a Thousand Miles* (Walker, 1984)

King Clive. *The Night the Water Came* (Harper, 1982)

Lasky, Kathryn. *Jem's Island* (Macmillan, 1982)

McElrath, William N. *Indian Treasure on Rockhorne Creek* (Broadman Paper; 1984)

Mayhar, Ardath. *Medicine Walk* (Macmillan, 1985)

Roberts, Willo Davis. *Megan's Island* (Macmillan, 1988)

Skurzynski, Gloria. *Caught in the Moving Mountains* (Lothrop,1984)

Steinbeck, John. *The Red Pony* (Bantam, 1959)

Nonfiction

Biological Sciences

Abbot, R. Tucker. *Seashells of North America: A Guide to Field Identification* (Golden Press, 1968)

Abbot, R. Tucker. *Seashells of the World* (Western, 1985)

Arthur, Alex. *Shell* (Knopf, 1989)

Blassingame,Wyatt. *Wonders of Sharks* (Putnam,1984)

Coup, Sheena M. *Sharks* (Facts on File, 1990)

Dow,Lesley. *Whales* (Facts on File,1990)

Eschmeyer, William N. and Earl S. *Herald. A Field Guide to Pacific Coast Fishes of North America: From the Gulf of Alaska to Baja California* (Houghton, 1983)

Graham, Ada and Frank Graham. *Whale Watch* (Delacorte, 1978)

Johnson,SylviaA. *Coral Reefs* (Learner,1984)

McGowen, Tom. *Album of Whales* (Rand McNally, 1980)

Morris, Percy A. *A Field Guide to Pacific Coast Shells, Including Shells of Hawaii and the Gulf of California* (Houghton, 1966)

Parker, Steve. *Fish* (Knopf, 1990)

Patent, Dorothy Hinshaw. *The Lives of Spiders* (Holiday, 1980)

Penzler, Otto. *Hunting the Killer Shark* (Rand McNally, 1981)

Shoemaker, Hurst and Herbert Zim. *Fishes* (Western, 1987)

Mexico

Epstein, Sam and Beryl Epstein. *Mexico* (Watts, 1983)

Marrin, Albert. *Aztecs and Spaniards: Cortes and the Conquest of Mexico* (Macmillan, 1986)

Rosenblum, Morris. *Heroes of Mexico* (Fleet, 1972)

Smith, Eileen Latell. *Mexico: Giant of the South* (Dillon, 1983)

Stein, R. Conrad. *Mexico* (Children's, 1984)

Answer Key

Page 10

1. Accept appropriate summaries.
2. This song means contentment and warmth of family and that everything is as it should be.
3. The Song of Evil came with the scorpion.
4. It was peaceful with a beautiful sunrise.
5. This word might have been used to heighten or to contrast the evil of the scorpion and the ensuing danger.
6. She was determined to see the doctor which was unheard of for the people with no money to pay for help.
7. Answers will vary. The doctor's neighborhood had walls around their houses, splashing fountains, and elaborate furniture. The fishing village had straw houses and dirt floors.
8. The doctor is a man who is used to indulgences and excess.
9. Kino is aware of the 400 years of prejudices and superiority of the doctor and his European born friends.
10. Racism or prejudice

Page 15

1. Accept appropriate answers.
2. He compares it to someone's nervous system.
3. He wants to know if he has any control over Kino.
4. He had a vision of how his old lifestyle could once again be attained.
5. They all wanted what the pearl would bring, yet it belonged to Kino.
6. He decided to have a rifle.
7. They both thought little of Kino, or Indians in general.
8. The Song of Evil surrounded the priest.
9. He buried it under his sleeping mat.
10. She thought it was a sin ... it was evil.

Page 20

1. Accept appropriate responses.
2. The whole town or appropriate response.
3. They would arrive at a price and all the others knew what it was beforehand. If called in to bid, they would underbid and say it was of little value. They were not independent, but all worked for the same man.
4. They did not want to bid so low so as to lose the deal.
5. They were killed or never seen again.
6. He was trying to point out that it was worthless.
7. They believed that the pearl sellers had not conferred with one another and were therefore telling the truth.
8. Go to the capital.
9. The dark music or the Song of Evil.
10. Someone bashes him in the head and attempts to steal his pearl.

Page 25

1. Accept appropriate responses.
2. She took the pearl and was going to throw it into the Gulf.
3. He was upset and took it back, forcefully.
4. A thief tried to rob Kino, and Kino killed him with his knife.
5. As a woman, Juana had the qualities of reason, caution, and self-preservation. These would save them.
6. She found that it had been searched and then set on fire.
7. He lets them stay in his straw house.
8. At one time Kino planned to cross the Gulf in his boat and go to the capital.
9. He might be killed or injured too.
10. He traveled north toward the cities.

Answe:r Key *(cont.)*

Page 30

1. Accept appropriate responses.
2. It was stormy.
3. It matched the turbulence going on with Kino and the whole town.
4. They left at night.
5. He broke off branches and swept his tracks clean. He also backtracked and walked in wagon wheel ruts so his tracks would be erased when a wheel ran over them.
6. He is convinced of the pearl's value because people keep trying to steal it.
7. When he woke up and saw the trackers in the distance.
8. A rifle. Just like he wanted from his profits from the pearl (ironically).
9. He gets shot by the rifle.
10. Kino threw the pearl back into the Gulf.

Page 42

Matching

1) pearl buyer 2) Juana 3) Doctor 4) Priest 5) Kino

True or False

1. False
2. False
3. False
4. True
5. False - He discovered the pearl's evilness at the end of the story.

Short Answers

1. She breaks from tradition and takes her sick son to the doctor.
2. The crowd is shamed because one of their own people lies for the foreign doctor.
3. They drew back out of fear.
4. It was an evil pearl.
5. Juana knew that it was Kino's to throw away as he was the one who found it. It symbolically meant that he finally came to terms with the pearl and admitted that it was evil.

Essay

1. Accept appropriate responses. Check that examples clearly support the writer's opinion.
2. She meant that she looked up to him. She would follow him anywhere, and he would die if necessary in his deterrnination to see something through. A quality that the author showed us repeatedly was that Kino would not be deterred by any obstacle. Juana thinks this in Chapter 5 after he beat her and took his pearl back.

Page 43

Accept all reasonable responses.

Page 44

Perform the conversations (dramas) in class. Ask students to respond to the conversations in several different ways, such as, "Are the conversations realistic?" or, "Are the words the characters say in keeping with their personalities?"

Answer Key *(cont.)*

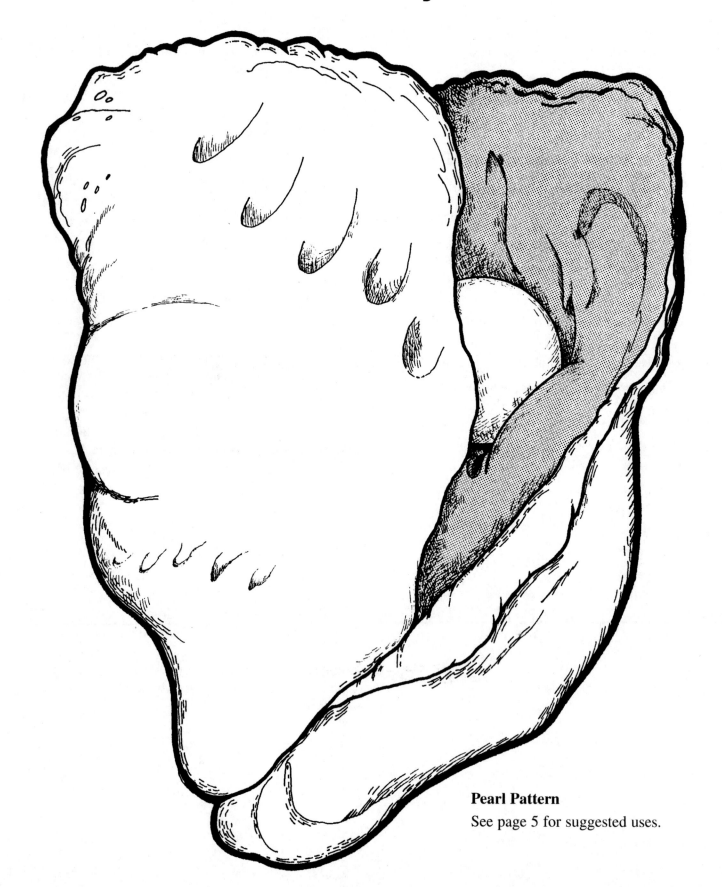

Pearl Pattern
See page 5 for suggested uses.